SACRAMENTO PUBLIC LIBRARY
828 "I" STREET
SACRAMENTO, CA 95814

7/2009

D1442066

DRAWING FANTASY ART

HOW TO DRAW
SUPERHEROES

Jim Hansen and
John Burns

PowerKiDS
press.
New York

Published in 2008 by The Rosen Publishing Group, Inc.
29 East 21st Street, New York, NY 10010

Copyright © 2008 Arcturus Publishing Ltd

All rights reserved. No part of this book may be reproduced in any form without permission in writing from the publisher, except by a reviewer.

Artwork and text: Jim Hansen
Colorist: John Burns
Editor (Arcturus): Alex Woolf
Editor (Rosen): Jennifer Way
Designer: Jane Hawkins

Library of Congress Cataloging-in-Publication Data

Hansen, Jimmy.
    How to draw superheroes / Jim Hansen and John Burns.
        p. cm. — (Drawing fantasy art)
    Includes index.
    ISBN-13: 978-1-4042-3855-8 (library binding)
    ISBN-10: 1-4042-3855-7 (library binding)
    1. Heroes in art—Juvenile literature. 2. Drawing—Technique—Juvenile literature.
I. Burns, John, 1947– II. Title.
    NC825.H45H36 2008
    743.4—dc22
                                    2007001479

Printed in U.S.A. by Bang Printing, Minnesota

Contents

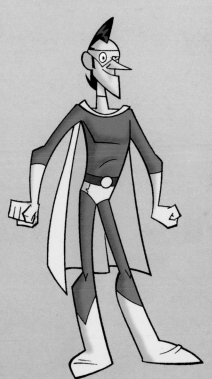

Introduction

This book will teach you how to draw superheroes in three very different styles: cartoon, screen hero, and manga. Whether you like your superheroes funny, tough, or cute, you should find a style here to match your tastes.

ARTWORK STYLES

Cartoon superheroes, like the one above, have greatly exaggerated proportions. You can have fun experimenting with this approach to create funny characters that are far from realistic.

Screen heroes, seen at right, are the tough, heroic, type of superhero you often see on TV. This book will help you create your very own superheroes to take their place alongside the many established ones.

Manga superheroes, at left, are known for their large, liquid eyes, and almost nonexistent noses. This delightful style, which originated in Japan, has inspired comic artists all over the world.

BASIC CONSTRUCTION

The bases of all comic characters are geometric shapes, such as squares, circles, and triangles.

When you draw these shapes, it helps to think of them as solid objects, such as spheres, egg shapes, cubes, and cylinders.

Now just juggle them in the right order and, presto! A new superhero is born.

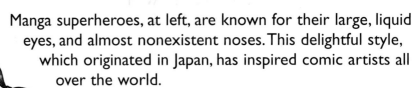

QUIPMENT

ood illustrations begin with good tools.
ather the following materials and equipment
efore you start drawing.

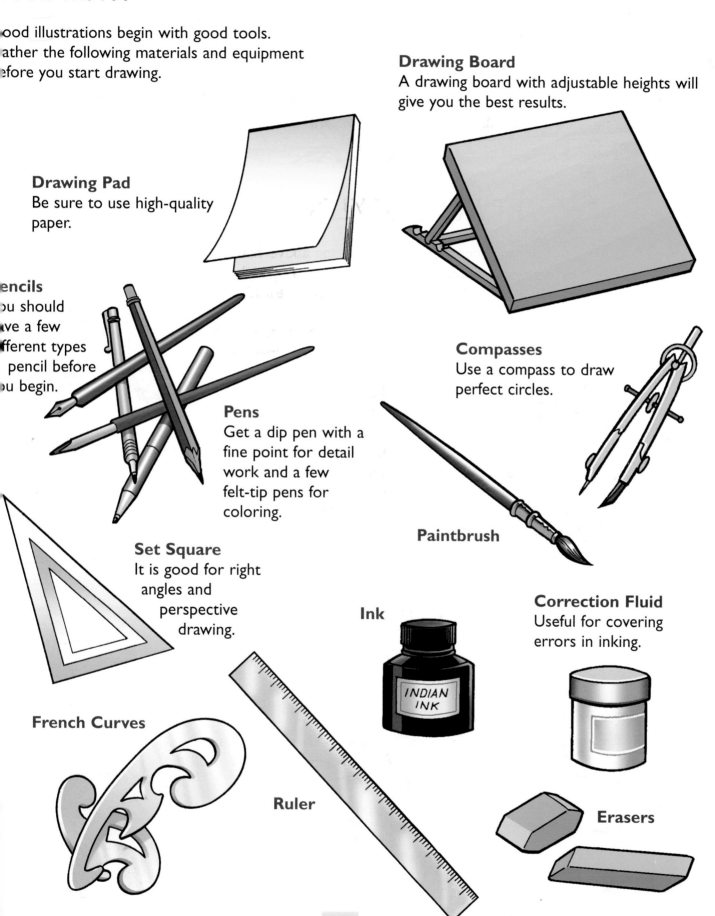

Drawing Board
A drawing board with adjustable heights will
give you the best results.

Drawing Pad
Be sure to use high-quality
paper.

encils
ou should
ve a few
fferent types
pencil before
u begin.

Pens
Get a dip pen with a
fine point for detail
work and a few
felt-tip pens for
coloring.

Compasses
Use a compass to draw
perfect circles.

Paintbrush

Set Square
It is good for right
angles and
perspective
drawing.

Ink

Correction Fluid
Useful for covering
errors in inking.

INDIAN INK

French Curves

Ruler

Erasers

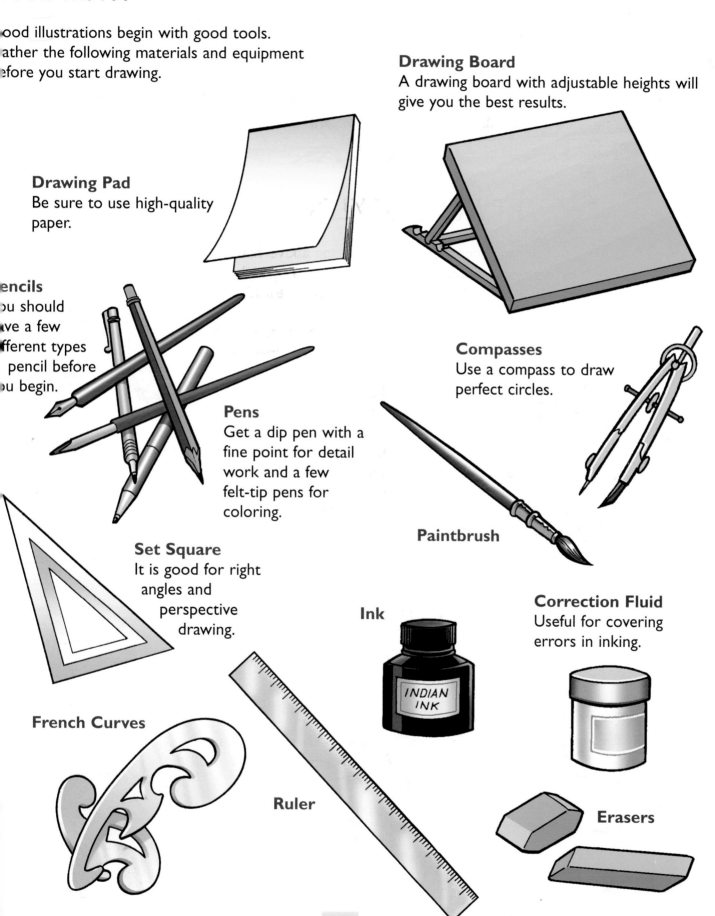

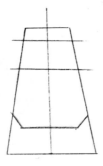

Cartoon Style

We will start with some fun drawings. There is nothing complicated about drawing cartoons. In fact, simplicity is the basis of this style. Grab your sharpened pencil and let's bring a few characters to life.

THE HEAD

Before you start on the body, create a face for your comic hero. It takes only four steps for your square-jawed superhero to be complete.

Front View

Stage 1
Draw the outline of the head, neck, and jaw.

Stage 2
Add the eyes, nose, mouth, and ears.

Stage 3
Fill in the details, such as eyelashes, eyebrows, and hair.

Stage 4
Finally, ink and color it.

Side View

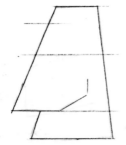   

s you have seen, the male cartoon hero is mostly made up of sharp angular
ies. In contrast, the female cartoon hero is drawn with soft curves.

ront View

Stage 1
Start with a
circle. Then add
the lower jaw.

Stage 2
Add the eyes,
nose, mouth,
and ears.

Stage 3
Fill in the details,
such as eyelashes,
eyebrows, and hair.

Stage 4
Finally, ink and
color it.

ide View

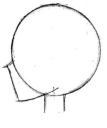  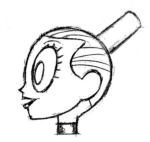 

Different angles

Here we view our female hero
from a three-quarter angle and
from below.

Notice how the guidelines for
her eyes follow the curve of
the head circle.

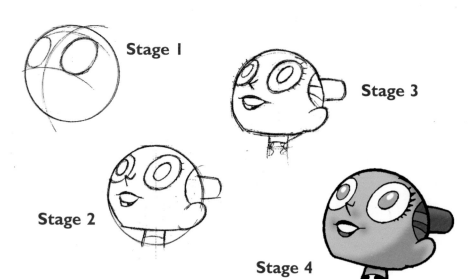

Stage 1

Stage 3

Stage 2

Stage 4

EXPRESSIONS

When you look at a cartoon, the face and its expression are the main focus of your attention. Giving your characters emotion really brings them to life. Here are just a few expressions for you to try drawing.

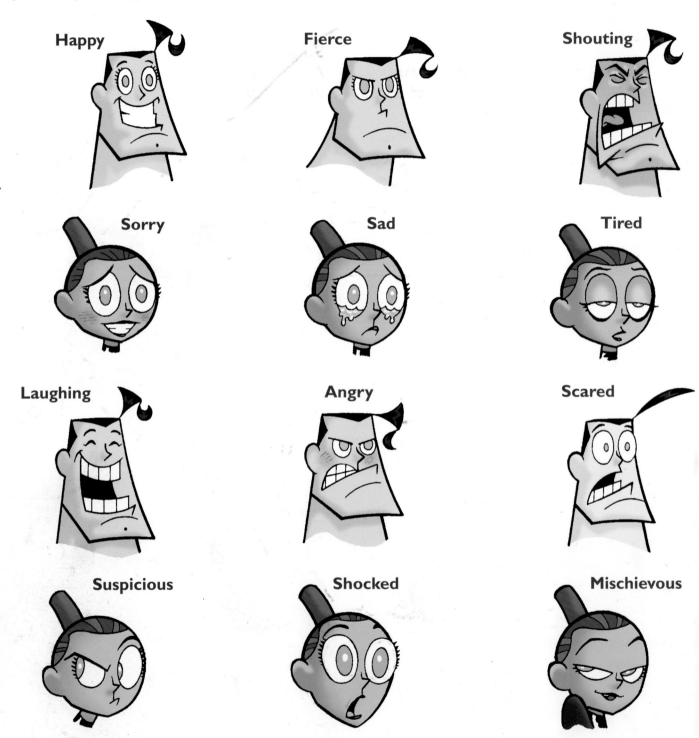

Happy

Fierce

Shouting

Sorry

Sad

Tired

Laughing

Angry

Scared

Suspicious

Shocked

Mischievous

THE BODY

All the geometric shapes come into play here. When drawing the whole body, start with a basic construction. Then build your shapes into a recognizable figure.

Male figure

Stage 1
Start with the basic shapes.

Stage 2
Add detail to the hands, face, and limbs.

Stage 3
Add in the hair and details to the costume.

Stage 4
Add some color.

Female figure

Stage 1
Use two ovals for her torso.

Stage 2
Outline her hair and facial features.

Stage 3
Add details to her face, hair, and costume.

Stage 4
Now add your choice of color.

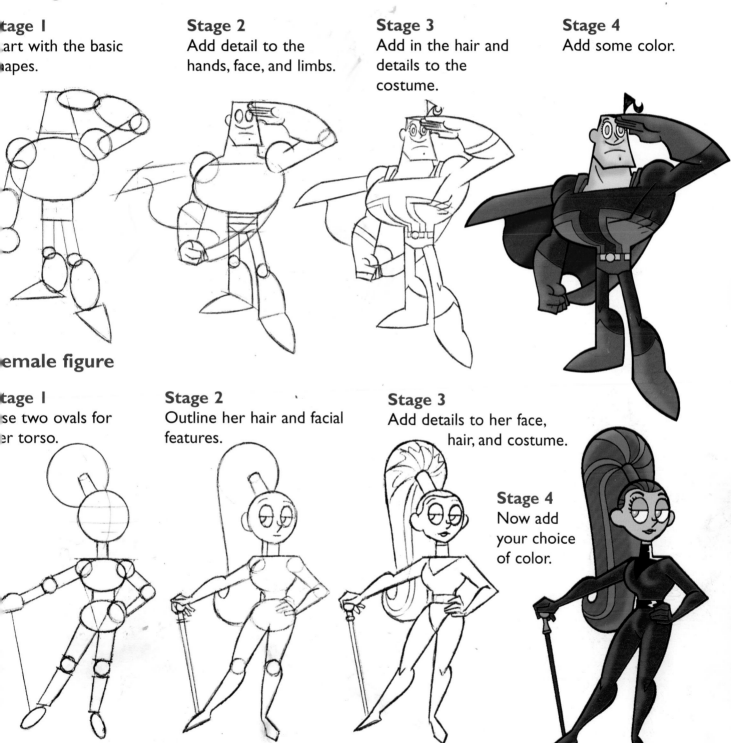

THE BODY IN ACTION

Now that we have gained some experience in drawing superhero heads and bodies, let's try putting them in action!

Stage 1
If you prefer, start off with a stick figure. Then add your geometric shapes.

Stage 2
Now shape his body, adding detail to his face, hands, and costume.

Stage 3
Finally, add ink and color.

Here is a three-quarter view of our superhero. We are looking at her from above.

Stage 1
Once again, start with a stick figure. Then add the shapes.

Stage 2
Shape the body, outline the hair, and add detail to the face, hands, and costume.

Stage 3
Now you can start inking and coloring.

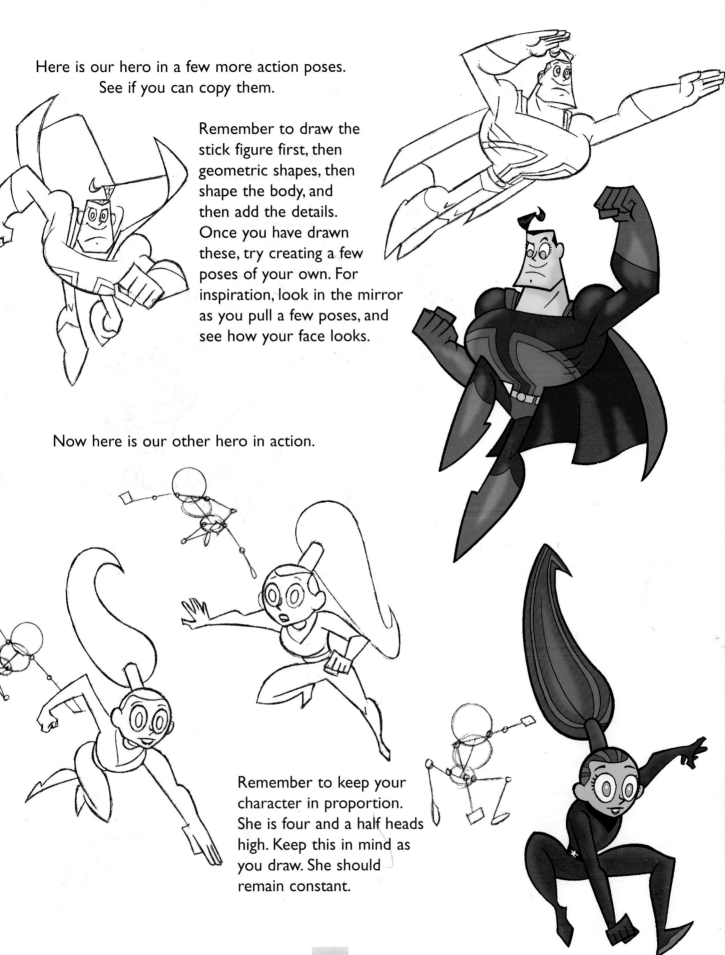

Here is our hero in a few more action poses.
See if you can copy them.

Remember to draw the
stick figure first, then
geometric shapes, then
shape the body, and
then add the details.
Once you have drawn
these, try creating a few
poses of your own. For
inspiration, look in the mirror
as you pull a few poses, and
see how your face looks.

Now here is our other hero in action.

Remember to keep your
character in proportion.
She is four and a half heads
high. Keep this in mind as
you draw. She should
remain constant.

DIFFERENT CHARACTERS: HEADS

In the cartoon world, the shape of a character's head often tells you a lot about his or her personality. Villains, for example, are usually either heavy and square or long and thin. You can play around with faces, eyes, noses, mouths, eyebrows, and ears. They can all be exaggerated. Experiment with different head shapes: pear, banana, round, and square.

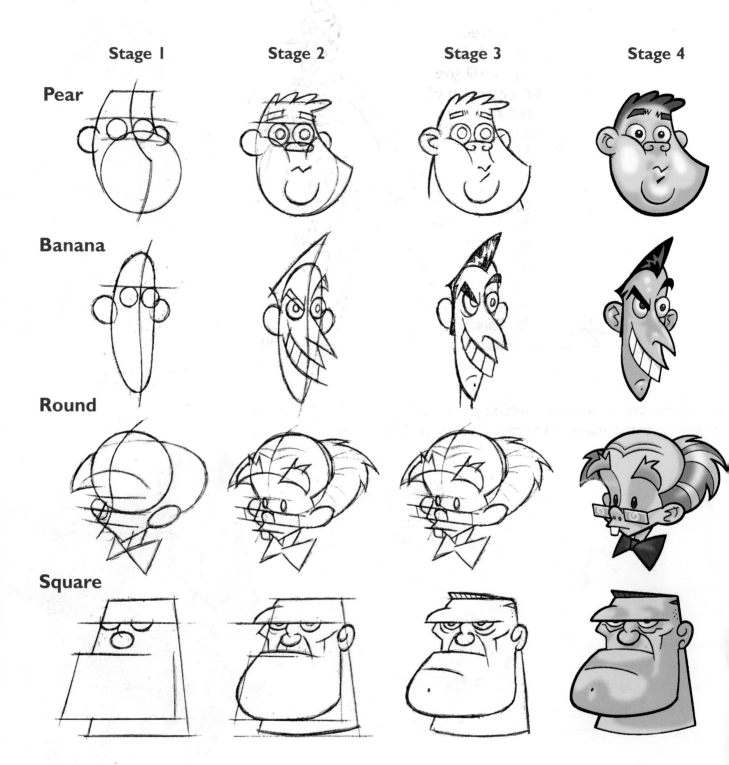

	Stage 1	Stage 2	Stage 3	Stage 4
Pear				
Banana				
Round				
Square				

DIFFERENT CHARACTERS: BODIES

ow that we have had some practice at drawing the heads of different
aracters, let's add the bodies. This one is a tall, thin villain. He has sharp, very
pinty features, so his figure includes a few triangles.

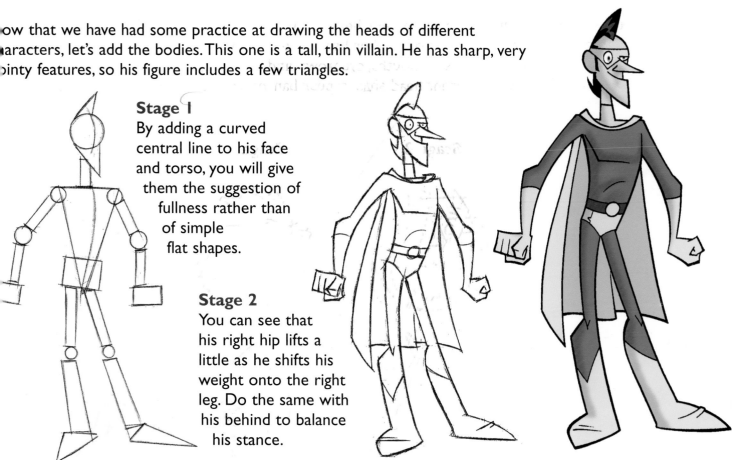

Stage 1
By adding a curved
central line to his face
and torso, you will give
them the suggestion of
fullness rather than
of simple
flat shapes.

Stage 2
You can see that
his right hip lifts a
little as he shifts his
weight onto the right
leg. Do the same with
his behind to balance
his stance.

Stage 3

or contrast, try drawing our villain's generously proportioned sidekick.
here are not too many sharp, angular lines on him!

Stage 1   **Stage 2**   **Stage 3**

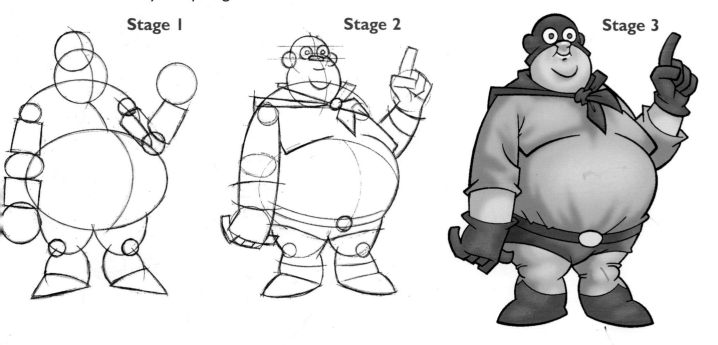

Screen Hero Style

In this section, we are going to learn how to draw the slick, stylized action heroes that appear on many children's TV programs. These caped crusaders can fly faster than a speeding bullet.

TEEN SUPERHEROES

First, we will look at teen superheroes. They tend to be slim, with narrow waists and small jaws.

Male

Our male teen hero is roughly five heads tall. We will draw him at a three-quarter angle, so his left foot is a little farther away from us than his right.

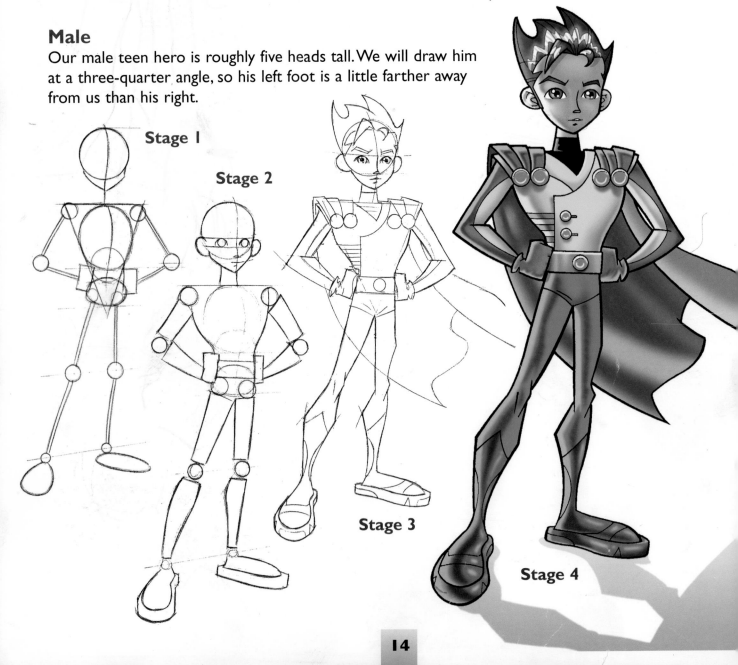

Stage 1

Stage 2

Stage 3

Stage 4

Female

The female teen hero is slightly smaller than the male and has a curvier shape, with a smaller waist and wider hips. She has an athletic build, and her arms are angular like the male's.

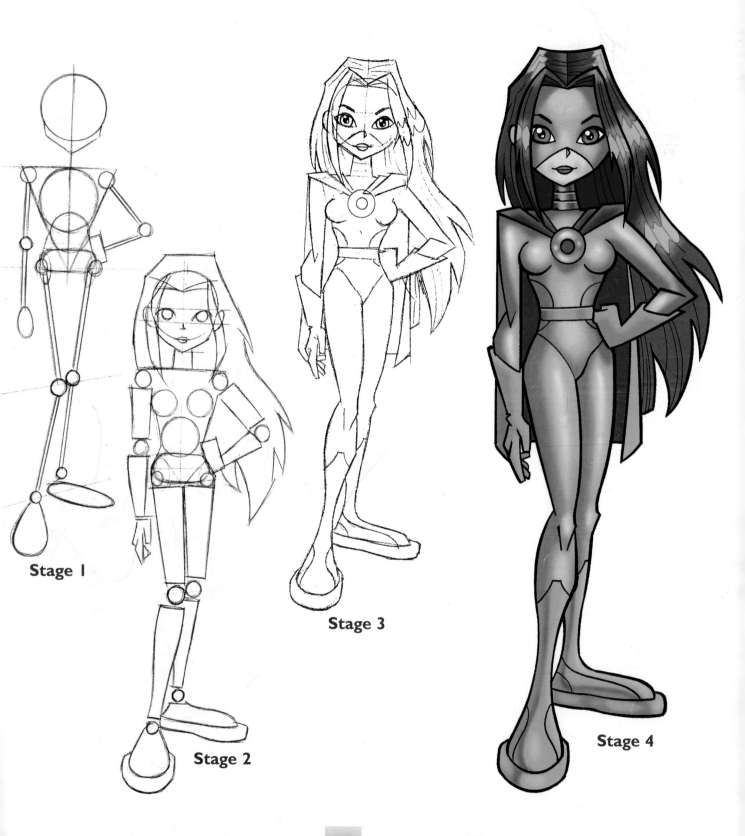

Stage 1

Stage 2

Stage 3

Stage 4

TEEN SUPERHEROES IN ACTION

Superheroes are always adopting dramatic poses. Starting with a stick figure and geometric shapes, you can draw the body in just about any position. Here are some examples.

Stage 1

Stage 2

Stage 3

Stage 4

In the early stages of your drawing, it is a good idea to draw an arrow through the body to show the direction in which it is traveling. This will help you balance the figure and make the pose look more natural.

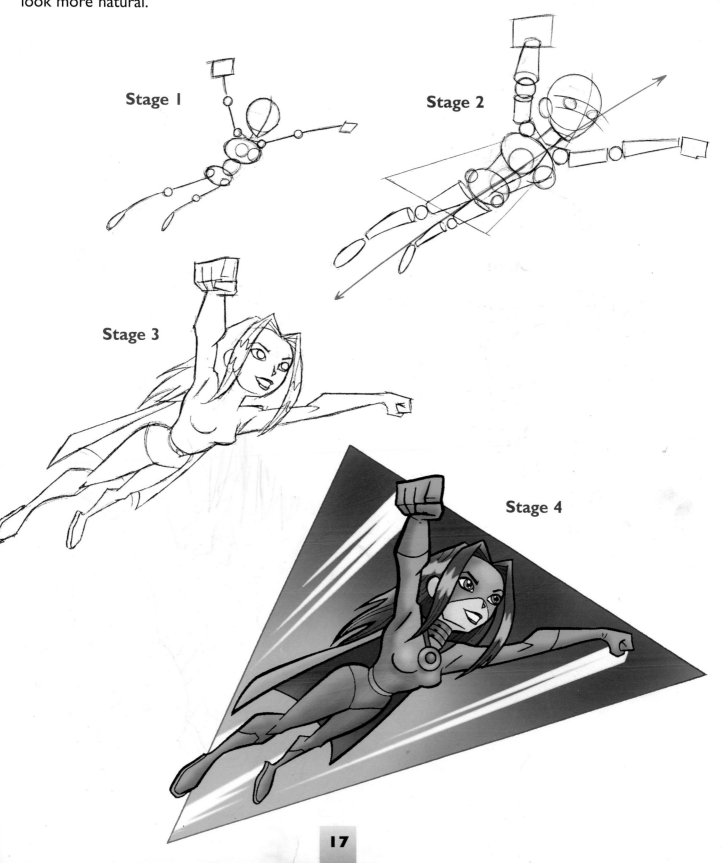

Stage 1

Stage 2

Stage 3

Stage 4

ADULT SUPERHEROES

The first thing you will notice about a male adult superhero is his size and bulk. The adult female is taller and also slightly curvier than her teen counterpart.

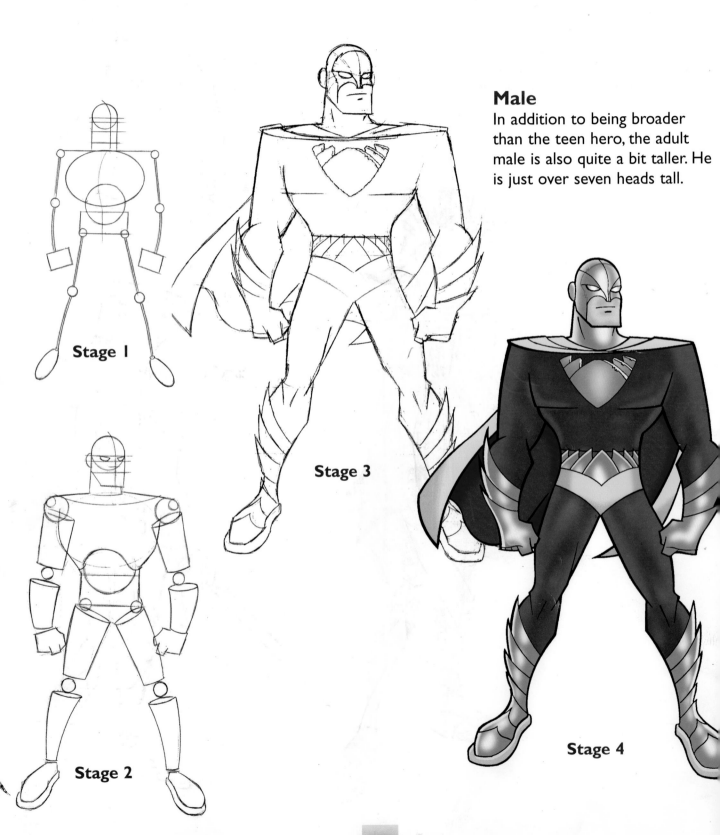

Stage 1

Stage 2

Stage 3

Stage 4

Male

In addition to being broader than the teen hero, the adult male is also quite a bit taller. He is just over seven heads tall.

Female

Note that the adult female has a smaller head than the female teen hero. Her eyes are slightly narrower and sharper edged, too. For this clean-cut style, keep the face simple. Do not add extra expression lines on her forehead or around her mouth. To change the expression, just raise her eyebrows, narrow or widen her eyes or mouth, and make her smile or frown.

Stage 1

Stage 2

Stage 3

Stage 4

ADULT SUPERHEROES IN ACTION

Now try to draw our heroes in fighting poses. Remember to always draw through. In other words, even when on part of the body is hidden by another part, make sure you always draw the bi underneath. This way you will know tha the limbs are correctly placed.

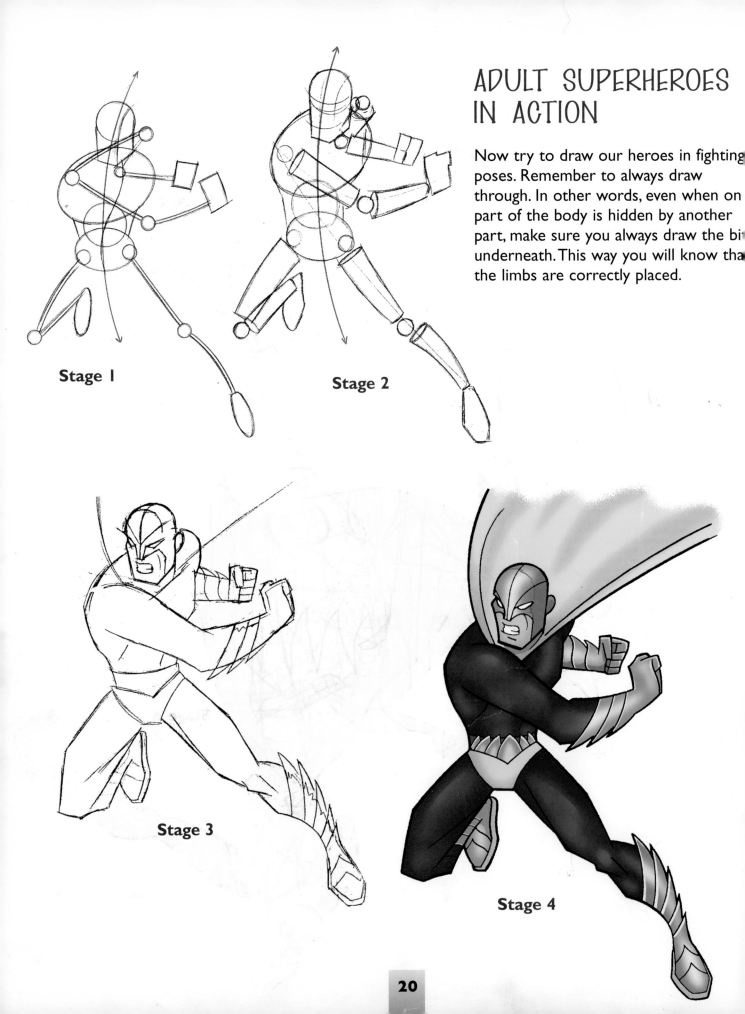

Stage 1

Stage 2

Stage 3

Stage 4

Stage 1

Stage 2

Stage 3

Stage 4

Manga Style

The key to good manga art is to keep your drawings simple. The pen line should be clean and smooth. Do not overwork your drawing. Adding lots of shadow and defining every muscle, hair, and wrinkle simply does not work with this style.

THE HEAD

Female

The head is very simple to construct. It is simply a circle with a jaw line added. Pencil in your eye level, with the top of the eye about halfway down. Then add the nose and mouth level.

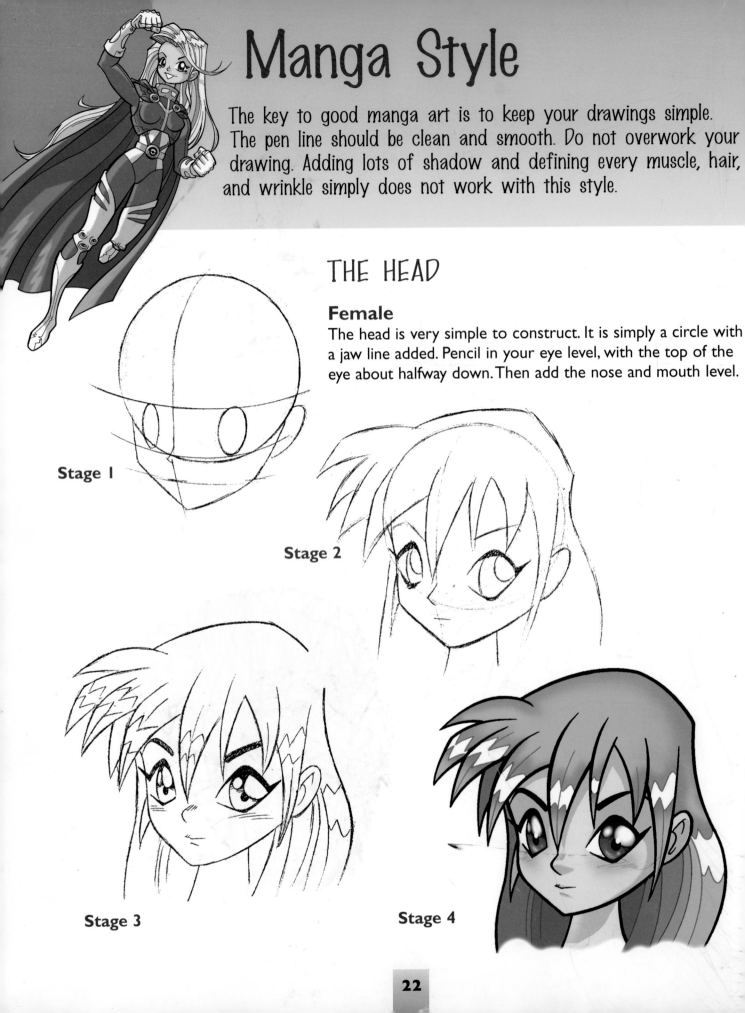

Stage 1

Stage 2

Stage 3

Stage 4

Male

The male head is constructed in the same way as the female head but with a square jawline rather than the female's *V* shape. The eyes are not as big as the female's, and there are no thick lines to suggest eyelashes. His hair is usually spiky and a bit messy.

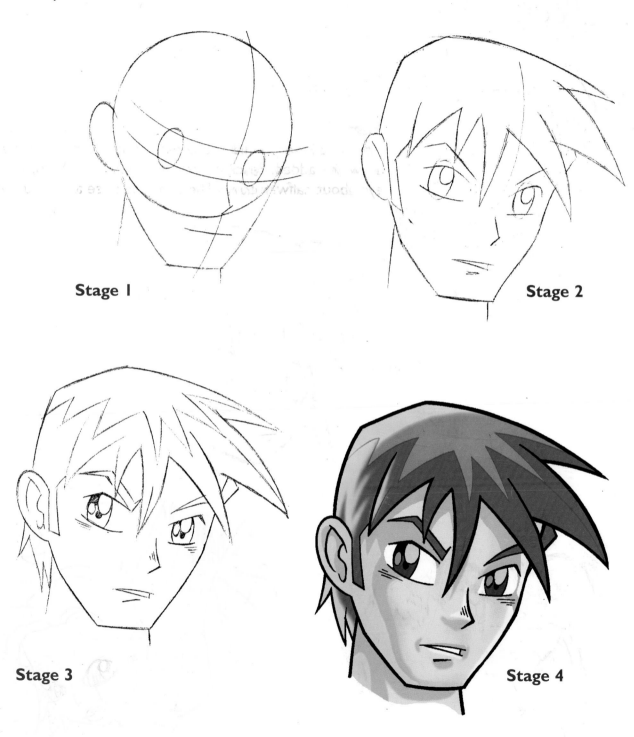

Stage 1

Stage 2

Stage 3

Stage 4

EXPRESSIONS

The face is the main focus of attention on the human body. It is the first thing we look at and it tells us far more than body language does. Words are often unnecessary, as the face says it all. Try out some of these expressions.

Female faces

Surprised

Angry

Playful

Enraged

Relaxed

Laughing

Bored

Sad

Curious

Male faces

Angry

Self-Important

Smiling

Suspicious

Embarrassed

Sly

Surprised

Scared

Shouting

THE FEMALE BODY IN ACTION

It is time to put our manga figures into action. We will try to draw them running, flying, kicking, and fighting. A good pose should suggest movement without the help of movement lines. Even in her fixed state, your character should look dramatic.

Try not to make your sketch too busy in its early stages. When you start to add the details, it could start to look quite messy. If you like, you can use a blue pencil to do your initial construction of ovals and circles. You may prefer to use a hard-lead pencil. Then you can switch to a softer pencil for the detailed stage.

THE MALE BODY IN ACTION

Now try the same with some male figures. Remember to draw through, as though the figure is transparent. In the kicking figure on this page, the hero's leg is in front of his arm, but you should still draw the arm in to make sure the proportions are correct.

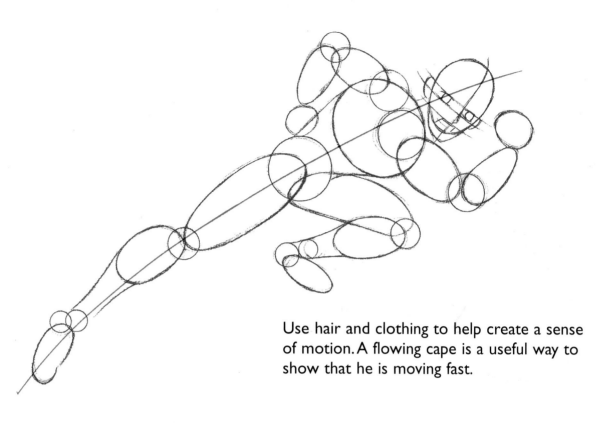

Use hair and clothing to help create a sense of motion. A flowing cape is a useful way to show that he is moving fast.

Glossary

angular (ANG-gyuh-lur) Having angles or sharp corners.

body language (BAH-dee LANG-gwij) Postures or movements of the body that may indicate a person's mood or state of mind.

clean-cut (kleen-KUT) Clear in outline or design.

cylinder (SIH-len-der) A shape with straight sides and circular ends of equal size.

define (dih-FYN) Show something clearly, especially in shape or outline.

dip pen (DIP PEN) A pen, usually with a replaceable nib, that must be repeatedly dipped into an inkwell when in use.

drawing board (DRO-ing BORD) A large flat board used for drawing. It can usually be adjusted to different heights and angles.

exaggerated (eg-ZA-juh-rayt-ed) Stretched beyond the truth.

facial (FAY-shul) Of the face.

French curve (FRENCH KURV) A piece of plastic with curved edges and curved shapes cut out of it to help illustrators draw curves.

geometric shape (jee-uh-MEH-trik SHAYP) A simple shape such as a square, circle, rectangle, or triangle.

manga (MAYN-guh) The literal translation of this word is "irresponsible pictures." Manga is a Japanese style of animation that has been popular since the 1960s.

perspective (per-SPEK-tiv) In drawing, changing the relative size and appearance of objects to allow for the effects of distance.

proportion (pruh-POR-shun) The relationship between the parts of a whole figure.

set square (SET SKWER) A thin, flat instrument in the shape of a triangle, used to draw lines at particular angles.

sidekick (SYD-kik) A companion.

sphere (SFEER) An object shaped like a ball.

stance (STANTS) The way a person stands.

stick figure (STIK FIH-gyur) A simple drawing of a person with single lines for the torso, arms, and legs.

stylized (STY-uh-lyzd) Drawn to achieve a particular artistic effect rather than to look natural.

torso (TOR-soh) The upper part of the human body, not including the head and arms.

transparent (trants-PER-unt) See-through.

Further Reading

Books

How to Draw 101 Superheroes by Hedley Griffin (Top That Publishing, 2005)

How to Draw Comic Book Heroes and Villains by Christopher Hart (Watson-Guptill Publications, 2001)

How to Draw Comics the Marvel Way by Stan Lee and John Buscema (Fireside, 1984)

How to Draw Manga Heroes and Villains by Peter Gray (The Rosen Publishing Group, 2006)

How to Draw Superheroes and Villains by Jael (Kidsbooks, 1995)

Step-by-Step Manga by Ben Krefta (Scholastic, 2004)

Superheroes: Joe Kubert's Wonderful World of Comics by Joe Kubert (Watson-Guptill Publications, 2000)

Web Sites

Due to the changing nature of Internet links, PowerKids Press has developed an online list of Web sites related to the subject of this book. This site is updated regularly. Please use this link to access the list:

www.powerkidslinks.com/dfa/shero/

Index